Reality Check

Reality Check

Charles Forrest

First Edition

Copyright © 2020 by Charles B. Forrest Jr.

All rights reserved, including the right of reproduction in whole or in part in any form except in the case of brief quotations embodied in critical articles or reviews. For permission, contact author at cbforrest129@gmail.com.

Printed on acid-free paper

ISBN 978-0-578-78874-6

dedicated to all the Saints who took time to teach me

Contents

Reality Check	3
God's Plan	9
Building Realistic Expectations	27
Understanding Ourselves	41
Our Role in God's Plan	55
Several Observations on the Nature of God	69
In Praise of Hard Times	81
Concluding Remarks	89
Epilogue	99
Notes	103
About the Author	105

We live in unreasonable times. But, of course, the times have always been unreasonable.

Do not seek revenge or bear a grudge against anyone among your people, but love your neighbor as yourself.
　　　　—Leviticus 19:18

Reality Check

And Jesus taught them to pray:

> *Our Father in heaven, hallowed be your name, your kingdom come, your will be done on earth as it is in heaven . . .*
> —Matthew 6:9-10

Try to imagine the number of people who have recited the Lord's Prayer. For over two thousand years it has been a mainstay in Christian worship across many languages. Today there are more than two billion Christians on the planet. Yes, God has heard this prayer request many, many times: *Your kingdom come, your will be done . . .*

But is this prayer really being heard? Does frequency numb the ear? Most Christians would say, "Yes, God hears our prayers." But more to the point, is it being answered? Some say yes, but many say no. We hear, I look around and it just doesn't look like heaven on earth to me. For whatever reason, I just don't think so.

The disconnect between our faith and what we see is frustrating. It questions our faith and our relationship to God. The fact is, many struggle with the idea that their prayers are not answered. This struggle can result in a weak, defensive faith and a poor testimony. We create arguments to reconcile this disparity. You've heard them, maybe my faith isn't strong enough and that is why my prayers are not answered. Or we may say, God knows best and He is working in our best interest. If God does not answer our prayer, then we must assume the answer is "No, not at this time," and God knows best.

Still, it is a simple question: "Is the Lord's prayer being answered?" If our faith is based in reality, we should be able to answer this question from direct observations. The answer should be verifiable by many people and be consistent over time. Even non-believers should be able to see the results from the prayers of so many Christians. Personally, if your relationship with God is based on reality, you should be able to see evidence of that relationship in your prayer life. Other people should be able to see it also. In other words, this evidence should be able to stand up to the close examination of Reality Checks.

Let's not get confused here. We are not questioning faith in God. Far too many saints have gone before us to put this issue to rest. The premise put forward here is that our understanding of prayer life is broadly too shallow, frustrating our ability to pray effectively and to see God's will being done. Ineffectiveness in our prayer life produces frustration resulting in the weak faith of Sunday/Easter/Christmas Christians. **Reality Check: Our prayer life should produce observations of God's will being done.**

This is a bold statement and undoubtedly one that will stir arguments from a broad spectrum. We Christians are a contentious lot. That's okay! But wouldn't you rejoice in seeing God's will being done and a fruitful prayer life? Allow me to outline the fundamentals for creating consistent, observable Reality Checks so that we can fully rejoice in our faith and avoid its frustrations.

> *We Christians are a contentious lot. That's okay!*

To see God's will being done, first, we must understand God's plan and our role in this plan. If we do not understand God's plan and what He expects from us, then we, as humans, tend to make things up. Being both creative and contentious, we not only have the ability, but the propensity to develop elaborate rules, rituals, and even gods to tell God what He can expect from us. Human created gods and rituals, however, result in legalism and a faith built on a poor foundation. Understanding God's plan and our role in it are critical to building a solid foundation and a fruitful prayer life. We will fully explore this in Chapter 2.

Second, we must have a realistic relationship with God so we know what we can expect from Him. Otherwise we may ask for things that are unrealistic or even contrary to God's plan for us. When we ask for something counter to God's plan and then blame Him for not giving it to us, our actions are counterproductive to building faith. Not only do we need to know what God expects from us, we need to know what we can expect from God. We will explore what a realistic relationship with God means in Chapter 3.

Third, we must understand ourselves and our inherent stumbling blocks to a fruitful relationship with God. We are humans every one of us. We often seem predestined to behave as we do because we share the same needs and desires, hopes and fears. Large numbers fail at marriage over the same behaviors. Large numbers come to Christ for the same needs and desires. And large numbers reject faith in God over shared fears. Even when we know better, (think of the alcoholic who knows drinking is not good for him, or the forgetful husband who knows he should make his wife a priority), we still struggle with doing the right thing, adopting the attitude we know we should adopt. In fact, it is quite easy to identify basic human responses that get in the way of a productive relationship with

God, and there are many, many examples from the bible we can draw on. We will take a look at these in Chapter 4. If we understand ourselves, we stand a better chance of getting ourselves out of the way so we can see God's will in action.

> *Know that the answers God gave me, may not be the exact same answers He gives to you.*

In the following pages, let me share with you the answers God gave me on my journey with the objective of establishing a realistic, more fulfilling faith based on God's will for us. Know that the answers God gave me, may not be the exact same answers He gives to you. That's okay. God calls us to a personal relationship based on our individual needs. Hopefully this book will inspire you to ask tough questions that refine your faith to a fuller and more rewarding relationship with God. Recall Jesus said:

> *For there is nothing hidden that will not be disclosed, and nothing concealed that will not be known or brought out into the open. Therefore consider carefully how you listen.*
>
> —Luke 8:17-18

A Thoughtful Moment

As we get started, let's think for a moment about where we are in our faith. There are devout Christians who call on Jesus each day. There are Sunday/Easter/Christmas Christians who are curious or want to expose their children to the benefits of Christianity. There are others, caught in the business of this world, who just do not have the time to think about Jesus. And, of course, there are those who call this nonsense and consider faith in God to be unenlightened.

Into which category do you fall? Why do you think that is? Please take a moment to write a sentence or two about where you are today and why.

You will find this book to be short, and it is short for a reason, which I will explain, but expect the journey to be worthy of your investment.

God's Plan

First, it is critical that we seek to understand God in light of His plan. He does have a plan and it is unrealistic to think we can have a productive prayer life without first considering what God expects from us. But before getting into God's plan, we must first deal with the blinding, often paralyzing stumbling block to our faith . . . disappointment.

Jesus disappoints a lot of people. We don't say it that way, of course. But when we first encounter the reality of Jesus, who answers prayers and performs miracles, we are overwhelmed. The mountaintop experience is incredible and we want that feeling to go on forever.

And we want more. Much more. We want to be blessed, to have our basic needs met for health, jobs, clothing, shelter, food, and transportation. We want to be liked and understood at home and at work. Who doesn't pray for these things?

We serve an all-powerful, all-knowing and loving God. Right? We know He can do these things for us. Yes, it's a disappointment when Jesus does not answer our prayers.

Take the Case of Beth

She was about fourteen, an only child, and a beautiful young girl when she fell on the stairs at school. It wasn't a bad fall; normally not an event to remember. However, the result of this fall was extraordinary. The nerves in her legs overreacted. They became incredibly sensitive. Over the next few years her life, her dreams, her activities were radically changed by that fall. Beth developed Reflex Sympathetic Dystrophy (RSD), a recurring pain syndrome. Today, this disease is more frequently referred to as Complex Regional Pain Syndrome, or CRPS. Her legs became extremely sensitive to everything. Even bedsheets caused unbearable pain. She dropped out of school and began seeing specialists. Over the years she endured all sorts of experimental treatments from powerful drugs to implanted portals fed by exotic needles. Some experiments were promising. Some even helped.

My wife and I met Beth's parents in Lamaze class and we both had beautiful baby girls about two weeks apart. Beth's father was a businessman and a politician on the local stage. Her mother was a former school teacher. Together, they made a distinguished couple. We became good friends and her father and I maintained contact over the years. We talked on the phone regularly and visited occasionally after business moved my family several states away when the girls were three years of age.

"Her legs are cold," her father was explaining one day, "and the doctors are worried that if we can't get the circulation back in her legs, she will lose them." I couldn't believe what I was hearing or even imagine having to say those words about my daughter. One day after another, year after year, the parents lived a life dealing with Beth's pain. Her father concluded, "She'll probably never live a normal life."

Because I am a father, I know the kind of hopes and dreams a father has for his child. They can be flexible, but they are always warm, positive, and hopeful. About the time my daughter was graduating from college, Beth got her GED and was thinking about technical school. She had a part time job as an aide in a nursing home. She wore a boot on one leg and got around on crutches. The people at the nursing home loved her and she enjoyed the work. With budget cuts and absences due to pain, however, the job did not last.

Out of the blue, a young man came into her life. Her father was naturally suspicious. Beth was beautiful and bright, with an infectiously wonderful attitude, but her medical condition portended a rough, expensive, and likely overwhelming future for any young man.

Not all things can be explained, however. The young man turned out to be a wonderful, caring, and patient suitor. In a few years they were married. The emotions that flooded her parents were overflowing. Hopes for a normal life for their beautiful daughter were suddenly possible. Hopes for years of fulfillment were conceivable. Beth wanted to have children but her parents knew her body would not support a baby through birth. Still, how wonderful it was to have "normal" worries!

Beth maintains many angelic qualities. She never complains. Her great smile and positive outlook get her through whatever test or experiment she is undergoing or whatever job she pursues. Beth spends a lot of time providing support and encouragement to perhaps thousands around the country with RSD through online support groups. Her faith in God is incredible. She is rock solid. Indeed, Beth may well be an angel.

Her father believed in God and that was a problem. He was bitter toward God for not healing Beth. I never once faulted him for that. We got together a couple times a year in a town midway between our homes. Whenever I mentioned religion, he cut the discussion off quickly. He knew there is a god and he knew God could have healed Beth if He wanted to. Lord knows enough people were praying for her.

When Beth approached thirty years of age. She lost all her hair. She lost so much weight her eyes stuck out.

Over the phone, her father told me, "You wouldn't recognize her. She always wears a hat. She . . ."

When Beth returned from Johns Hopkins Medical Center in Florida, we learned the nerves in her stomach are dead. The walls of her large intestine are smooth. Her body was not absorbing the nutrition necessary to sustain life. She faces a future dependent on a feeding tube... or not.

"I feel like the doctors told her she was going to die without giving her a time," her father said. Demonstrating her perpetual positive attitude, her father continued, "She told me this is just one more thing for me to get through." Beth is incredible.

One can hardly imagine the anguish Beth, her husband and her family go through each day. Yet we know from history that terrible things happen and they are happening still. It has always been so. Some people are suffering mightily at this time and their friends and families are fighting to keep faith in God for the time they are given. Jesus does not always answer their prayers. Yes, Jesus disappoints a lot of people, and as a result people can become bitter and resist knowing God better.

Are we destined to bitterness, resentment, disappointment? Or worse, are we only suitable for a naïve and weak faith? What is our role in this? Let's take a moment and look at this reality from another perspective, one that hopefully makes more sense.

Remember that, like us, Jesus had his struggles. Harsh struggles not of his own choosing. Recall Jesus said, "Father let this cup pass from my lips . . . "

> ## A Grace Moment
>
> How did you feel when I said I didn't fault Beth's father for being bitter toward God? Do you fault the father? Did your sympathy for the father suddenly decline because he questioned God? It's okay. God made us and He knows our weaknesses and proclivities. God can handle our questions and even judgments while we struggle to know Him better. God is a patient teacher and guide for those who seek His answers. Never forget, God delights in our freely choosing to love Him, even if it is with our last breath. Let's get back to up front and personal struggles.

Perhaps it's time for a Reality Check. Our bodies are subject to trauma, disease, aging, and the need for nourishment. If we step off a tall building or get hit by a speeding car, it can get messy. If we are exposed to disease, we can get sick. We grow old. We die. We know this. We see it. It's verifiable and it's consistent across time. It is our reality.

We sincerely pray to God for protection and for healing when we need it. We engage others to pray for us and we say this is a good thing to do. Can God answer these prayers? Yes. Sometimes He does. Miracles happen every day, but more often than not, Jesus does not intercede in the way we pray for him to. Even when he does, and there is a miraculous healing, in the end the person still dies. Indeed, death can be the way Jesus chooses to heal someone, but that is rarely what we pray for.

> *Death is part of the Plan.*

Some die young, seemingly without consideration of their potential, their goodness or even for those left behind. **Reality Check: No matter how religious or faithful, we all share the same fate.** We know this to be true because we see it happen. It is evident that our faith and prayers are not meant to alter this reality. Such unanswered prayers are not Jesus's fault. Suffering and trials have a purpose. Death is part of the Plan.

God's Plan

Our faith and prayers do not alter this reality for one good reason: God's Plan. What is this plan and what is our role in it? What can we realistically expect from God?

The Apostle Paul explains it best, and his answer is consistent from Genesis to Revelation. Paul draws this bold conclusion:

> *I consider that our present sufferings are not worth comparing with the glory that will be revealed in us.*
> —Romans 8:18

What would cause the Apostle Paul to dismiss our earthly reality so easily? What will be revealed in us that makes it okay? Paul explains God's Plan in Romans chapter 8:

> *[22]We know that the whole creation has been groaning as in the pains of childbirth right up to the present time. [23]Not only so, but we ourselves . . . groan inwardly as we wait eagerly for our adoptions as sons. [20]For the creation was subject to frustration, not by its own choice, but by the will of the one who subjected it . . . . [19]The creation waits in eager expectation for the sons of God to be revealed.*

Who subjected the creation, and likewise us, to futility and decay, temporal bodies? God did of course. It is part of his plan.

Frustration and decay. Pangs of childbirth. Why would God subject us to that? Paul's explanation was definitely not covered in my Sunday School lessons as a child. But now, as adults, we are forced to reconcile what we witness from Reality Checks with the reality of God as explained in the Bible.

The Apostle Paul began his explanation with "We know . . . ," as in we all know this foundational truth to be the basis of God's Plan and the platform on which to build our faith and our lives. In Romans 8:28, Paul explains that we face these trials so we can have the opportunity to be revealed as children of God with rights to an inheritance.

This, this is the glory that will be revealed in us, that we become children of God. This is the platform from which Jesus, Paul, David, Peter and our ancestors based their hope and daily focus.

What glory indeed! If we transition our perspective from disappointment with daily strife to hope in being revealed as children of God, we witness one of God's greatest blessings simply through understanding His plan!

Paul continues in verses 26-27:

> . . . [T]he Spirit helps us in our weakness.
> . . . [T]he Spirit intercedes for the saints in accordance with God's will.

God is pulling for us! He is waiting for us, like an expectant father, to be revealed as His children with all the rights and privileges of heirs and worthy to spend eternity with Him. If we call on God, we come to the inescapable conclusion and eventual acceptance that God is in control. Not us. **Reality Check: It is God's Plan that's important, not our plan.** This is a hard word.

We want God to bless our plans. We pray to God to answer our prayers to accomplish our plans. Unfortunately, this is not God's Plan and he is in control. If we focus on our plan, we are going to be disappointed in God and frustrated in our prayer life.

We are assigned a key role in God's Plan that no one should claim is easy, haphazard, or meaningless. It is none of these things. Our role is important and, as we will see later, incredibly challenging: we must fulfill our role based on faith, without knowing when our time on earth will end. Our role is meaningful, potentially rewarding, and filled with promise of blessings in the midst of our present sufferings.

> *It is God's Plan that's important, not our plan.*

To fulfill our role and be confident of God's blessings without a script requires faith, but not blind faith. The challenges are real but not overwhelming because, as we just learned, God is pulling for us and the Holy Spirit is there to intercede for us. In later chapters we will explore more fully exactly what our role entails and what we can expect from God.

It is God's Plan that explains why so many turn to God when they are down and out, and overwhelmed by daily struggles. We were made to turn to God in response to the challenges and pressures of the earthly realm.

As Christians, we possess God-given advantages and significant powers that non-believers do not possess. We must learn, however, to use these gifts and be quick to take advantage of the aid they provide. These gifts include:

> Fulfilling the need in our hearts to love God
> Accepting Jesus as the example to follow
> Accepting forgiveness for our sins
> Receiving the Holy Spirit to strengthen, guide, and intercede for us.

God hopes, He anticipates, and He expects (three great verbs from different translations) that each of us will be revealed as His child during our stay on earth. He gave everyone a need in their heart to find completeness from God. He sent Jesus as an example, and Jesus was sacrificed on the cross for our sins to make our consideration for adoption by God even a possibility.

A Grace Moment

If you are a non-believer and have made it this far, I'm surprised. Much of this probably sounds like mumbo jumbo, though I've worked hard to avoid jargon. Don't think twice if some of the references and words seem strange at this point. That's not the important thing. These concepts will become meaningful to you in your time. The important thing is taking stock of where you are in your life. Remember, most Christians you meet were once non-believers also. The fact is, most people start out as non-believers and it has always been that way. Keep reading and asking questions. Just don't plan to be among those who go through their entire life without seriously considering the reality of Jesus. Let's get back to the plan.

Growing old is not for wimps. We will need to rely on the Holy Spirit more each day to strengthen, guide, and intercede for us as the challenges of life intensify. While God made it clear he is pulling for us and giving us what we need to be revealed as his children, bottom line is that it is up to us. The challenges we face are part of our reality because they are part of God's Plan.

This plan is a hard word for many. Some reject the idea that God would test us altogether. Others reject a god who would create such a plan. You have every right to question and reject this plan. You are free to reject it. No one can force you to accept it. I doubt anyone will even try. It's your choice. As you compare your reality with the plan laid out in this section, however, consider also the following verses from the Bible:

> *In the beginning, God created the heavens and the earth.*
> —Genesis 1:1
>
> *God saw all that he had made, and it was very good.*
> —Genesis 1:31

The reality we see around us is part of God's Plan. Our role is to respond to this reality in a way to be revealed as children of God.

Isaiah affirms God is in control and that our role is part of his plan in these familiar verses:

> *All men are like grass,*
>   *and all their glory is like the flower of the field.*
> *The grass withers and the flowers fall,*
>   *because the breath of the Lord blows on them.*
> —Isaiah 40:6-7

God addressing Israel:

> *See, I have refined you, though not as silver;*
> *I have tested you in the furnace of affliction.*
> *For my own sake, For my own sake I do this.*
> —Isaiah 48:10-11

The Apostle John adds:

> *Yet to all who received him (Jesus), to those who believed in his name, he gave the right to become children of God— children born not of natural descent, nor of human decision or a husband's will, but born of God.*
> —John 1:12-13

The Apostle John wanted to make clear that there is a difference between those revealed as children of God and those who are not!

> *This is how we know who the children of God are and who the children of the devil are: Anyone who does not do what is right is not a child of God; nor is anyone who does not love his brother.*
> —1 John 3:10

God is in control. This is perhaps the hardest dimensions of faith to grapple with. We may pray for blessings and to be protected from curses, but God is in control and we have to accept it. God made the creation and set it in motion. As a result, we now have the opportunity to be revealed as children of God, or not.

Returning to the original question for a moment: *does God hear and answer our prayers to build the Kingdom on earth?* We can now conclude it is up to us to build the Kingdom on earth and thereby be revealed as children of God.

As evidence, we can look around and see the wonderful benefits of good leadership: advances in medicine and longevity, more people being fed and lifted out of poverty, and greater justice throughout many lands. Likewise, we see the degradation and hopelessness resulting from bad leadership and the selfishness of bad and greedy people. Fortunately, we know God is pulling for us to be revealed as His children. He provides everything we need. We have a choice. It is up to us.

Throughout history, the lives, writings, and decisions of many biblical characters and our ancestors reflected this understanding of God's Plan and their role in it. Expectations were largely focused on perseverance to fulfill their mission.

Today, many of our leaders want better government but lack the Biblical perspective of God's Plan.

Therefore, we have lost much of the understanding required to see God's will in action, and, as a result, have paid a huge price in the loss of personal satisfaction, declining morals, and loss of real freedom. Fortunately, we know with God, it is never too late.

Understanding God's Plan sheds light on what a proper relationship with God looks like and what God expects from us. In the next chapter, we'll take a look at what a realistic relationship means in terms of what we can expect from God.

A Grace Moment

A psychology professor was giving his testimony at a New Canaan Society meeting one morning. He said, "I was one of those teachers who taught your children that God didn't really exist; that throughout time man has invented a god to explain the events in their lives that they didn't have an explanation for." He continued, "I figured this out all on my own!"

We had a laugh. He then told the group of about two hundred men how he came to know the reality of Jesus.

A Thoughtful Moment

But what if you reject this reality? What if Paul is wrong? Paul was not perfect and there are a number of contradictions in Genesis we cannot explain. And we don't hear anyone else talking about this plan. Okay, God made the heavens and earth and everything in them, and Jesus died on the cross for our sins, but that was enough. Since then, if we worship God, give, be good, pray for things we need, God's blessing will be upon us. Right? It will rain on our fields. Our family will be healthy and prosperous, or at least better off than the non-believers. Right? All the advances in science, medicine, and inventions will come from Christians. Right? Look around. How does this view fit with your reality?

If God had asked me, things might be a little different. I would like to make some changes. My god would be a little less ambivalent toward the rust and decay part; preferably tending toward less rust and decay, at least for the faithful. Things would also be fairer. Obviously, some people suffer much more than others. Some are born with or into handicaps that make life harder through no fault of their own. That is just not fair.

The length of time it took to be revealed as children of God would also need to be revisited. Perhaps our time on earth would be much longer, or as I think about it, perhaps we could be raptured as soon as we are revealed as children of God. That would avoid the problem of backsliding. What changes would you make?

We hear people say, "I could never worship a god who allows such atrocities . . . or a god who condemns my friend because he is gay . . . or a god who would allow my child to suffer and die from cancer/car wreck/murder/abuse/hunger . . . or a god who allows the innocent to suffer . . . or a god who allows my father to be stricken to bed suffering day after day for twenty years . . . ."

What limits do you have in mind for your god?

Building Realistic Expectations

We can expect God to be God, uncompromising and in full control of his plan. We now also see that it is not realistic to expect or hold out for Jesus to sympathize with our egocentric arguments or answer our prayers if they conflict with His plan.

Studying our relationships with others can provide insight to what we can expect from God.

Building Trust, Avoiding Fantasy

We hopefully have close personal relationships with our parents, spouses, children, and friends. These relationships are real and we understand that our words and actions have consequences within these groups. Further, we have expectations, usually realistic ones, of what we can and should be able to anticipate from these relationships. You may know better than to ask a friend for $100,000 to invest on a stock market tip, but you are confident about asking your spouse to pick up dinner on the way home from work. We get surprises from time to time, but for the most part we know those close to us well enough to know what we can expect. **Reality check: We need to know God well enough to know what we can expect from Him.**

Sometimes we fantasize about relationships. I may go out to pick up wine and appetizers for a romantic evening at home with my wife who I think is crazy about me, when, in reality, she's been meeting with an attorney and plans to announce our divorce that same evening. Ouch! My actions do not reflect our reality and are apt to result in great disappointment! Later, I may rationalize why I was wrong, or more likely why she was wrong, and things did not work out between us. Most of us tend to rationalize situations in a way that reduces our pain. It's human nature.

Once disappointment sets in, however, there is little incentive to plan a future around broken faith. Whether our rationalization is right or wrong, we tend to avoid building our lives around anything that greatly disappoints us. We know from experience how critical it is that our relationships be based in reality if they are to function successfully.

Fantasies and misconceptions, for all their fun and promise, are eventually proven wrong. And when they are, we must choose to either live in disappointment or sincerely re-evaluate our thinking to establish a more realistic relationship. A realistic relationship is one in which we understand where the other person is coming from, what they expect of us, and what we, in turn, can expect from them. **The relationship must also be one we choose to pursue.** If we do not choose to pursue it, the relationship will never become meaningful. We must be purposeful and determined in our pursuit of knowing God if we are to avoid fantasy and disappointment.

Further, we do not relate to just physical relationships. We also live in a world of intense feelings and emotions. **Emotions are real even if they are not true.** The sting of a perceived slight is real, even if the slight was not intended. Although we cannot see the emotion, we can describe it and anticipate that certain emotions have real consequences. Like the wind, we can observe an emotion's effects and even describe the results to others. We can even gain agreement among a broad group of people, consistently over time, to observations of people's emotions such as "she is so in love" or "he is really angry."

> *We must be purposeful and determined*

Likewise, we bring our individual experience, expectations, and fantasies to our relationship with God. If we have a relationship with God based on an unrealistic understanding of what God wants from us or unrealistic expectations of what we can expect from God, it will not be a rewarding or productive relationship. Further, if we fantasize about our relationship with God, we are bound to be disappointed; if not at first, then eventually. Fantasies and misconceptions can be sustained for a long time, but eventually they will prove false and lead to disappointment. Once disappointment sets in, our commitment becomes lukewarm, our prayers perfunctory, our testimony weak. We know something is missing and the excitement we felt when we first met Jesus is long gone.

At this point, we have a choice. **We can live in disappointment with a weak faith or we can strive for a relationship based on reality.** Once we comprehend our role, we have a more realistic understanding of what we can ask for and what we can expect from God. This understanding provides a solid foundation for a rewarding and productive relationship. We must choose to search for and live in a relationship with God based in reality to avoid broken trust.

Does this mean our relationship with God must be perfect? Of course not! Just as with our earthly relationships, misunderstandings are evident even in the best of marriages, work situations, and classrooms. These misunderstandings must be worked through, lessons must be learned, and forgiveness must be extended. Of course, it is best to carefully avoid broken trust if at all possible. This requires work. A half-hearted, lazy pursuit will not get you to a rewarding relationship.

Prayer is the most foundational aspect of our relationship with God. It is helpful to seriously study our relationship with God as we go to Jesus in prayer. God is patient and understanding. Further, we have the Holy Spirit to intercede for us. Having a relationship based in Reality is important because it will lead to a fruitful prayer life, thus confirming that we are on the right path and reinforcing our desire to know God better.

For most of my life, prayer consisted of petitioning God for his intervention. Namely, asking Him to do something directly: help me get a job; protect my family; bring about world peace. God was somehow in need of my petition to do His will on earth. My prayers confirmed that God has the power, that He knows what needs to be done.

> *In my name or His?*

As long as I was praying to God to do something, I believed I was doing my part. I could leave church on Sunday knowing I had done my duty with prayer and petitions to make this a better world. The minister had done the same. The minister and I have done our part by praying for a better world. Right? I can feel good about myself. Right?

Well maybe not entirely. **Reality Check: If I'm not getting the expected prayer results, maybe, just maybe, my understanding of how this relationship works is the problem.** I can fantasize about how God needs my petitions a bit longer, but it is hard to see why I should expect different results.

After studying God's Plan, we can see why simply petitioning God to do His will on earth may not be productive. His plan calls for us to be about His work to His glory to be revealed as His children both worthy of an inheritance and desirable to spend eternity with.

Jesus rarely petitioned God to do things. Jesus was a laborer, not just an observer! Jesus prepared himself for ministry, gathered disciples, developed an organization, and left home to teach and heal. Then Jesus went to the cross. He worked to do His Father's will for His Father's glory. Imagine if Jesus never left the synagogue, but instead stayed in the synagogue praying and studying scripture and teaching. Surely Jesus's prayers and teaching would have been awesome . . . but would God's will have been done?

Jesus said:

> *Let your light shine before men, that they may see your good deeds and praise your Father in heaven.*
> —Matthew 5:16

Maybe we are supposed to be laborers also. When we pray, "Thy will be done," we are praying for God to bless the "works of my hands" to do His will on earth much in the same way Jesus prayed, regarding the cup of crucifixion, that God's will, not his,

> *It is up to us to build God's Kingdom*

be done. Jesus prayed for God's will to be done, knowing that it was he who would be hanging on the cross. We are to do the same now that we know that just praying to God to do something is not enough. Like Jesus, we must be laborers, not petitioners. **Reality Check: We can conclude it is up to us to build God's Kingdom on earth.**

Seeing God's Will in Action

While God has intervened in my life several times to let me know beyond a shadow of a doubt that He cares, I have not found any consistency in His answers to my prayers when I am praying for myself. In other words, when I pray in my name, I may or may not get an answer. Just ending the prayer with, "in Jesus name I pray," does not change the fact that I'm actually praying for my will to be done. I am praying in my name.

But when I pray in His name, in other words, for "His will to be done," I can show some predictability and consistency in terms of answered prayers. For example, I teach financial crisis clients how to manage their money and their debts. When I turned attendance over to God, the classroom filled up. I reach out to clients and follow up by being diligent. I prepare and teach as creatively and earnestly as I can, but it is God who is changing lives. I'm just being diligent. I'm helping His children in His name to His glory, not mine.

Viewed in this light, we see incredible things being done in the name of Jesus and for the glory of God. We see good people feeding and sheltering the poor daily; prison ministers and AA leaders changing lives one person at a time. We see missionaries commissioned and the good news of Jesus being preached in all corners of the world. Bibles are being distributed. Individuals and governments are working to provide clean water, sanitary conditions, and medical help to the needy all over the world. When we leave church after saying the Lord's Prayer, the focus must be on what we are doing to bring about God's will on earth. **God's blessings are very real and consistently revealed when we have a realistic relationship with God.**

In Apostle John's later years, he explained this understanding of effective prayer very clearly, writing:

> *This is the confidence we have in approaching God: that if we ask anything according to His will, He hears us. And if we know that He hears us, whatever we ask—we know that we have what we asked of Him.*
> —1 John 5:14

The Apostle John focuses on "His will"; not our will. Again, it is God's Plan that is important, not ours.

> ## A Grace Moment
>
> Take your time here. Think about the implications these paragraphs contain for your faith. The Apostle John is revealing to you a source of real power and boldness in this verse. There is no ambiguity in John's statement. This power is for you. It is available to you today but this power is not for your will. It is not about fulfilling your plan. But it is awesome, real, fulfilling, rewarding, and meaningful. Further, you may be able to see it at work today!
>
> In the Old Testament, the phrase "His Name" meant the essence of, or actual, God. For example:
>
> > *Then go to the place the Lord your God will choose as a dwelling place for His Name.*
> > —Deuteronomy 26:2-3

God's Gifts

Let's explore another topic that hinders a realistic relationship with God. God's idea of "giving" and "blessing" seems to be different than what we learned as children. It is instructive that in the Old Testament, God promises to give the Israelites a land of "milk and honey." He made this promise to Abraham and again to his heirs. The promise was repeated often. But many years later, when Joshua led the Israelites across the Jordan into the Promised Land, they had to fight for every foot using weapons they made with their own hands years earlier. Not exactly my idea of a gift! But in the context of God's Plan, God gave Joshua and the Israelites the land by giving them the opportunity to do His will. God wanted them to have the land, thus demonstrating the power of their God to the entire world.

God's "gift" required considerable faith and obedience before it could be received. In the Book of Joshua, within six sentences, God told Joshua to "be strong and courageous," not once, but three times. And then God added, "Do not be terrified; do not be discouraged." Was God concerned that Joshua might fail? That God's promise to Abraham and his heirs might be in jeopardy? That the Israelites might sit back and wait for God to round up everyone in the Promised Land and bring them before Joshua to surrender?

No! Failure was not a consideration. Joshua, like Paul and Jesus, had a realistic understanding of what "gift" meant. Each knew what their role was and what they could expect from God. They knew God's will would be fulfilled. Today, too many petition God for blessings and sit back waiting for the phone to ring, or a mysterious check to come in the mail.

God's gift was a mission to do God's will for His glory. And it had a promise attached: that God would give Joshua success if he was faithful. Joshua was given a mission for God. God put him through many years of trials, doubt, hard work, and struggles to prepare him for the task. Undoubtedly, God took many more years than Joshua would have preferred, and this time and work required a lot of faith on Joshua's part.

Unlike Joshua, we may not know what our mission is until circumstances develop and there we are. But always remember, when Joshua crossed the Jordan, he had a large, well trained and tested army, the Ark of the Covenant, AND the Angel Commander of the Army of the Lord helping him. God had Joshua fully prepared for success!

Are we willing to accept our gifts and blessings? The Israelites still had to fight for the land using cunning and skill. And so it is with us. If we are doing God's will, in His name and not our own, it may be hard, it may take a long time, require a lot of preparation, faith, even drudgery, but failure? No way. We are laborers for a master planner. There are many examples in the Bible of God's extensive preparation to achieve His will.

When we pray to God for Him to do something for ourselves, we are praying in "our" name. We are praying from our perspective that our plans be blessed. It is possible that God is putting us through some particular challenge to prepare us for his purpose. Praying to remove this challenge may well be contrary to God's will. But when we pray to God for things in "Jesus" name, i.e. according to Jesus's will, we are praying from God's perspective for His will to be done and for His glory. When we pray in Jesus's name, for something he wants us to do, we open the door for His blessings to flow in. We are also praying about what we can and will do for Jesus and the glory of God. We are not praying for our will or our project. It is God's Plan and project that are important. We are just being diligent.

Try to avoid self-serving thoughts here. I remember a time shortly after accepting the Lord, I was flying to New York on business and after seeing an ad in a travel magazine, it occurred to me to pray to God to win the lottery. I could use the money for good projects and ten percent straight to the church—a win-win outcome! Right?

A Grace Moment

We must not be afraid to challenge our faith with the tough questions and be persistent in seeking answers that make sense in light of what we can know. As adults, we are forced to revisit concepts such as Gifts and Blessings versus the reality of God's will and promises. God can handle the questions, and our faith will be better grounded for asking them. It might just require some digging and praying to get the answers you seek but do not settle for answers that do not pass a Reality Check.

A Thoughtful Moment

Some argue it is a matter of faith that God hears and answers every prayer. If we do not receive an answer, then we must assume God said "No," and said so in our best interest. God knows better than we do what we need. Further, we are to bring everything to God in prayer, petitioning Him to do something, and, of course, He can do what He wants to do. Right? What we are praying about is not the important thing. Right?

When Jesus said, "And I will do whatever you ask in my name, so that the Father may be glorified in the Son," the emphasis is on, *I will do whatever you ask*, and the *in my name* part is just a reminder we are praying to Jesus, right? What is your reality in regards to these prayers?

Also, does saying we must be laborers for God rather than petitioners for Him to bless our plans imply salvation by works, not faith?

Understanding Ourselves

We Christians are a contentious lot. When studying a realistic relationship with God, it is helpful to examine some of the stumbling blocks common to our human nature that prevent us from doing our part in the relationship. Identifying these stumbling blocks will help us see them for what they are: barriers to a productive relationship with God.

The Human Response

Okay, we want to be revealed as a child of God. And we want to have a realistic relationship with God: a child of God doing his Father's will. If you have read this far, you have probably accepted this by now. But what does a child of God do? Fortunately, God sent His son as an example of what we should do in a clear, easy to understand manner. But before we get to exactly how children of God spend their time in Chapter 5, we have to deal with another reality: The Human Response. The Human Response is a basic, almost instinctive human answer to God's commandment to love Him: We want to know what's in it for us. Furthermore, this benefit has to be something we actually want. As Job postulated when arguing with his friends:

> *Who is the Almighty that we should serve him? What would we gain by praying to him?*
> —Job 21:15

We must understand how The Human Response affects our thinking before we can be expected to think and act like Children of God. After all, what could be more natural than to think, "If I am worshipping an all-powerful, all- knowing and loving God, He will take care of my most basic needs and protect me from catastrophe"? Right? If not, what's the point of stretching for the Kingdom?

This Human Response need not surprise anyone! And don't be too quick to say, "Not I!" We quickly learn from the Bible that the Human Response has always been so. After Jesus fed the five thousand near Bethsaida, many tracked him to Gennesaret on the other side of the lake hoping to be fed again. You can almost hear them say, "Free food! Man, I'd follow you anywhere." These followers were intrigued by Jesus's message, but what they really wanted was a free meal. Jesus could see what was in their hearts.

Were these people bad? No! They naturally saw something in Jesus they wanted: free food! But the focus on the free food kept them from grasping Jesus's true message for their lives.

There are many examples of the Human Response in the Bible. John the Baptist foretold of the Messiah:

> *His winnowing fork is in his hand, and he will clear his threshing floor, gathering his wheat into the barn and burning up the chaff with unquenchable fire?*
> —Matthew 3:12

Does that sound like Jesus of the New Testament? Well, no. Jesus came as a Teacher and performed miracles to support his claims and to encourage people to believe in him. But he didn't beat anyone with a stick or burn the Romans with unquenchable fire as the Jews were hoping the Messiah would do.

Was John the Baptist disappointed with Jesus? Well, yes. Jesus was not acting the way John the Baptist anticipated. So, John the Baptist sent his disciples to Jesus to ask, "Are you the one or should he wait for another?" Even though John the Baptist had been told the "one on whom the spirit of the lord descends" was the Messiah and John the Baptist saw the spirit descend on Jesus like a dove, he still questioned if Jesus was the Messiah because Jesus did not fulfill his belief of what the Messiah was supposed to do. We have the same problem today. Many hold strong points of view as to who Jesus is supposed to be and what he would or would not do. It's part of our Human Response.

A Grace Moment

Let's detour for a moment. Did John the Baptist's questioning of Jesus make him a bad person or a person of inadequate faith? No! Remember, God made us. He knows our weaknesses and proclivities and stands ready to forgive us many times over as we struggle to know Him. God can handle our questions. Let's get back to another Biblical example of the Human Response which we still find today.

Toward the end of Jesus's ministry, during Passion Week, Jesus entered Jerusalem a hero, drawing huge crowds. He had just raised Lazarus from the dead. Lazarus was from a well-known and respected family that lived only a few hours walk from Jerusalem.

Lazarus had been dead several days when Jesus raised him. Several Priests were present, paying their respects along with other visitors and family, when they witnessed the resurrection. There could be no question about the miracle. Jesus was the Messiah, and, by the time he entered Jerusalem, most everyone knew it.

Yet by Wednesday, only three days later, the crowds were becoming disillusioned. Jesus taught about the Kingdom of God and love but he did not talk about revolution and returning the kingdom to Israel, which the Messiah was supposed to do. The people turned away from Jesus and finally turned him over to the Roman authority. Even in light of clear and verifiable evidence, raising Lazarus from the dead, Jesus was rejected because he did not fulfill the people's need and expectation that the Messiah would free them from Roman rule.

> *How could they have been so blind?*

We ask, "How could they have been so blind as to reject Jesus as the Messiah?" In reality, this rejection happens all the time. We become so focused on our own problems and needs, we reject the god who does not answer our prayers for relief. We create our own criteria for a god who will bless us and fix our problems and reject a god who "rejects" us. But, as we see from God's Plan, this is not a realistic approach to God, and can only result in frustration and disappointment.

The Apostle Paul and Barnabas learned the hard way that people do not take kindly to gods who disappoint them. While preaching in Lystra, Paul healed a man who had been crippled from birth. Witnesses concluded Paul and Barnabas must be gods and began preparing sacrifices to them. Paul and Barnabas were alarmed at the thought and assured them they were humans like themselves. The people, enraged at "being tricked," stoned Paul and dragged him outside the city gates, leaving him for dead!

The crippled man was healed, but Paul was bloodied and bruised. People do not respond well to a god who disappoints them.

Even in light of objective, verifiable, and powerful evidence, we can and often will reject "truth" if it does not address our Human Response. Not because a miracle did not happen. Not because Jesus is not who he says he is. Not because the event or miracle introducing us to Jesus is not spectacular. No! But because Jesus did not fix what we desperately want—healing for a loved one, return of an estranged spouse, freedom, revenge, justice, food, etc.—Jesus is rejected.

One of the most heart wrenching examples of this phenomenon is found in Acts 1:6. Shortly after Jesus was raised from the dead, one of his followers asked, "Lord are you at this time going to restore the kingdom to Israel?" Living under the heel of harsh Roman rule was such an all-consuming burden, it was difficult for this man to focus on the miracle standing in front of him. Jews desperately wanted, needed and prayed for a military savior. But that was not Jesus. They were disappointed. Looking at Jesus—the man who John the Baptist proclaimed to be the Messiah, the man whose friends and enemies alike witnessed raising Lazarus from the dead and who himself just arose from the grave—in the eye, his follower asked, "Are you going to meet my need and drive the Romans out and return the kingdom to Israel?"

God's perspective is different than ours. The Israelites so wanted a military Messiah to overthrow the Romans, but God didn't defeat the Romans for another 300 years, when in AD 313–337, the Roman Emperor Constantine professed Christianity and set the stage for the faith to spread throughout the empire and subsequently the world. No one predicted this, and it definitely wasn't on the Israelite's timetable. Christianity began to spread based on God's timetable.

We are so concerned with our own earthly problems. We cry, "Lord, Lord," but keep him out of our hearts because our hearts are focused on our problems. We pray to Jesus, in our name, and cling to disappointment when our problem does not get fixed. The Human Response: to be so absorbed with our own situation and problems that we do not see or even want to take the time to understand God's perspective.

Rick Warren said it well in his book, *The Purpose Driven Life*: "It's not about you." As much as we want God's will to be about us, however desperately, it's not. **Reality Check: Jesus did not come to drive out the Romans. He may well not be here to fix your most pressing problem.**

An Unexpected Turn in the Road

Life can be brutal at times. If our alcoholism, drug addition, depression, depravity goes on long enough, we often hit what is called "bottom". We've come to the end of ourselves and we give up and call out in pain. When your vision closes in, your heart aches, your eyes fill with tears, and you just want the pain to go away, instead of relief, you come face-to-face with a choice. The choice that arises seems at first, most improbable. You are introduced to the concept of TRUST. It is strange that when we come to the end of ourselves and fall on our knees, we come to the issue of trust instead of faith, friends, or even hate. Trust runs counter to our Human Response but choosing trust opens the door to building a realistic relationship with Jesus and to developing an understanding of what we can expect from a loving and expectant Father. Immediately and inexplicably we find the relief we seek through Trust. Disappointment melts away. It is impossible to achieve Trust as long as we are disappointed in Jesus.

That is why it is important to understand our Human Response so we can turn instead to God's Plan for our lives and learn Trust. The Psalmist, David, understood this well when he wrote:

> *Trust in God at all times, pour out your hearts to him, for God is our refuge.*
> —Psalm 62:8

Take the Case of Grady

Grady was a young boy in the neighborhood where I grew up. He was a problem child. If something mischievous happened, grown-ups assumed Grady did it. One day Grady told me all the trouble didn't bother him because, "God looks out for us crazy people." I came to understand Grady did not mean he was crazy but that he lived in a crazy world far beyond his control. Grady knew from his mother that Jesus was looking out for him even when no one else would or could.

Grady's father was an alcoholic. The father had spent time in jail for cutting a man and he bragged about preferring a small knife. The father was often drunk. Grady never knew what to expect when he came home. One weekend, the father drove his truck into the ditch in front of the neighborhood store for everyone to see. It stayed in the ditch for several days until the father sobered up enough to get someone to pull it out. It was embarrassing, but worse, without family transportation, there was no way for the father to get away from the house and give the family a respite. Grady lived in a crazy world in which he could only hope to survive. His mother's faith was rock solid and she was in constant prayer for Grady.

Sometimes we find ourselves in a crazy world that is beyond our control. It's the pits, and few people handle it well. But we can pray to God and trust in Him to take care of us in Jesus's name. Grady survived and his mother's faith eventually saved the father. It was a tough childhood and it wasn't pretty, but Grady trusted that Jesus would look after him, and Jesus did. Grady did not pretend to know or understand Jesus, but he had a childlike trust in his mother's faith.

If we are doing God's will (in his name, not ours), working as his children to the Glory of God, then we can Trust God to take care of us. Jesus says so. Plus, there are sufficient testimonies for the merits of Trust to at least provide a platform for taking the first steps. Christian fellowship is critical to journeying in Trust.

It is instructive to look at what Jesus and Paul prayed for as examples of what we can expect. Jesus prayed for His father's will to be done, miracles for the Glory of God, and protection for His disciples. We do not get any sense of Jesus praying for himself or his glory, or for basics like food, shelter or clothing.

Despite all Paul's hardships and the misgivings of other church leaders, he did not pray for material things or his stature in the church. Paul prayed for strength and perseverance to face the trials given to him in order to fulfill his mission and for the churches he mentored.

There are, however, at least one example each where Jesus and Paul prayed for themselves. Jesus prayed not to be crucified (not to have to drink from the cup of crucifixion), but that God's will be done. Paul prayed that "the thorn" in his side be removed, but again, only if it was God's will. Note that God did not grant either of these prayers. Still, Jesus and Paul rejected The Human Response and trusted God. They were content putting God's will first.

We must learn to identify how our Human Response shapes our hopes and desires. Then we can reject egocentric arguments and prayers to seek a God-centered perspective and pray "in Jesus's name" rather than our own.

Having dealt with the issue of the Human Response and its impact on our ability to Trust God, let us turn back to "what does a child of God do?" in the next chapter. Specifically, what is our role in God's plan?

A Grace Moment

We Christians are a contentious lot! So, let me clarify, I am not saying we should not pray to God for whatever we need even if we pray in our name. After all, we do have the Holy Spirit interceding for us and it may be to God's glory to grant his children blessings. We can pray for our needs without fear because we are His children. He made us and He understands our struggles with the Human Response. Just keep in mind God's Plan for you and your objective to be revealed as a child of God. Whereas prayers in Jesus's name (to accomplish his will) can show great consistency for Reality Checks, prayers in our name, for our own needs, have a lower probability of fulfillment. The reason for this is prayer in our name may not be compatible with God's Plan for us.

A Thoughtful Moment

Okay, but does trusting in Jesus actually put meat on the table? I've got a family to feed. Are you saying I can quit my job, join a ministry, and trust God will somehow feed my family?

What do you think?

Anyway, isn't life about being selfish either way? I mean whether we are worried about this life and focused on our current problems or we are worried about our eternal life and focused on getting to heaven, aren't we still focusing on me, myself, and I in either case?

How would you respond to this person?

Our Role in God's Plan

We see that our objective is to be revealed as children of God and we pray for strength, guidance, and perseverance to do God's will. But what do we actually do? What is our role in this? We are a busy people. Our time is filled with work, children, social commitments, and church. We go to church. We pray. We give. Isn't that enough?

Today, most people are distracted by the necessity of money, how to get it and what to do with it, so let's talk about money first. There is no shortage of people saying you should give more. Give till it hurts! There are budgets and projects that need our time and particularly our money. Stewardship season stretches from fall around to summer these days. We ask, "Did I give enough? Am I doing enough? What would be enough?"

Of course, our role as children of God is not about money. **Reality Check: God does not need our money.**

God is not broke. He is looking for sold out Christians, not money. We all know this. Further, there is little to support the idea that simply giving or receiving money will get you into Heaven. Where is the excitement of doing God's will in writing a check? A church business manager once told me, "People actually undergo two conversion experiences. First, they undergo a conversion of the heart. Sometime later, they undergo a conversion of the pocketbook!"

> *God is looking at our heart*

God is looking at our heart. The church business manager was right. Once there is a conversion of the heart, the pocketbook will take care of itself. The key point is that money is a cheap substitute for actually doing something solely for the glory of God.

Before listing activities, let's begin with a little framework for evaluating our role as children of God. Understanding his commandment to love one another is key to doing God's will here. This will allow us to look at what Jesus actually did and told his disciples to do, and see how these activities might apply in our lives today.

Seeing the Face of Jesus

Christians look to Jesus as a role model to be emulated. Thankfully he is a worthy model in every way. Jesus was a teacher by both words and action. One of the best examples of "Go and do likewise" is found in the gospel of John:

> *He (Jesus) saw a man blind from birth. His disciples asked him, Rabbi, who sinned; this man or his parent's that he was born blind?"*
>
> *"Neither this man nor his parents sinned," said Jesus, "but this happened so that the work of God might be displayed in his life. As long as it is day, we must do the work of him who sent me.*
> —John 9:1-6

Jesus healed the blind man.

The man was born blind so that Jesus could heal him, demonstrating the work of God on earth to God's glory. The blind man then saw the face of Jesus. Jesus is painting a clear picture here of our role in God's Plan.

It's natural to imagine ourselves being mighty men and women of God, doing great things to help those less fortunate. But in reality, and given our Human Response and struggles, there are times in each of our lives when we look to others for help, encouragement, and accountability. In other words, there will be times when we are the "Blind Man" in this situation, looking for someone, in the role of Jesus, to come along and help us for the Glory of God. **Then we see the face of Jesus in others.**

Likewise, given these same conditions in others, there are times when we are the face of Jesus and we take on the role of healing the "Blind Man" for the Glory of God. In short, there are ample opportunities as we journey through life to be both the face of Jesus for others and to be helped by others for the Glory of God. **When we see life this way, God's Plan provides a never-ending stream of opportunities to both give and receive for the Glory of God, thereby fulfilling God's will on earth.**

One year, a recovering alcoholic may be receiving help for his addiction and the next year he may be a counselor helping another struggling alcoholic overcome his addiction. In the process of giving and receiving, a person has the opportunity to be revealed as a child of God. God's Plan is clever, indeed, and often surprising!

Take the Case of the Autistic Boy

One Youth Sunday, a young man recounted his missionary experience in Haiti. He told of sitting on a stone wall with an autistic boy at a beggar's orphanage on the side of a mountain. The autistic boy placed his hands on the young man's face and made earnest, guttural sounds. "I must be like the face of Jesus to this boy," thought the young man. Then he paused and a wave of emotion suddenly overwhelmed him, "It was then I realized his was the face of Jesus to me."

Take your time here. Re-read the last few paragraphs, for this section speaks to the plan's requirement for humility and peace. Here we learn how to see God's will unfolding on earth, and the bricks and mortar of the Kingdom.

Let's take one more step in tying our role and God's Plan together. In the gospel of John, Jesus talks with great clarity about God's will and Jesus's specific role. Listen:

> *All that the Father gives me will come to me, and whoever comes to me I will never drive away. For I have come down from heaven not to do my will but to do the will of him who sent me. And this is the will of him who sent, that I shall lose none of all that he has given me, but raise them up at the last day.*
> —John 6:37-39

There is nothing ambiguous in Jesus's statement. Jesus is very clear about his role and mission. Don't listen to people who will tell you what Jesus "meant to say" in this passage. You can read this for yourself.

In the process of giving and receiving, we are building the Kingdom and helping Jesus fulfill his mission.

When, in John 14:13, Jesus says, "And I will do whatever you ask in my name, so that the Son may bring glory to the Father," he really means it! Jesus wants to answer your prayers **in his name** to bring glory to God, thereby fulfilling his personal role; a role given to him by God.

Reality Check: Jesus's role is now our role. When we help Jesus fulfill his role, we are also fulfilling our role to bring glory to the father. Read this verse again:

And I will do whatever you ask in my name, so that the Son may bring glory to the Father.

Let me boldly state it is of no benefit to compare our efforts to what others do. A wise businessman once counseled me, "Everyone knows some people contribute more than others, but that's not the important thing [to the success of a company]. The important thing is that everyone contributes what they can."

After a lifetime in business and reflecting on the great and mediocre leaders I've known, this philosophy appears to be both wise and true. I believe it is the same in the Kingdom of God. The important thing to the success of the Kingdom is that everyone contributes what they can. People are born with different gifts, and in different environments, directly impacting what they can contribute. This is not a surprise to anyone, least of all to God who made us. He knows the gifts and abilities we are given, and only God can weigh the merits of one's contributions. As in business, if everyone pulls together and contributes what they can, surprising and outstanding success is not only possible, it is highly probable.

We each have the opportunity to be the face of Jesus for others, and, at times, to see the face of Jesus in others. Go and do likewise for the Glory of God both giving and receiving. Not for our own benefit, but that God's will be done on earth and Jesus's role on earth is fulfilled. We cannot buy our way into a right relationship with God, but we can be about demonstrating our worthiness to be called a child of God. And, as we are being revealed as children of God, we serve as examples and encouragement to others. God's Plan is clever, indeed!

> *Go and do likewise*

But What does a Child of God Actually do?

Maybe it's time for another Reality Check. Is such a scenario of giving and receiving realistic in these modern, impersonal times? After all, talking about Jesus can get you kicked out of a lot of schools today. And, *Welcome!* isn't the expected response when knocking on a neighbor's door to say, "Jesus sent me." There are even some street corners in America where you can be arrested for disturbing the peace if you handout Christian literature. Indeed, it is responsible to be careful when considering giving and witnessing in public. Let's face it: there are some good reasons not to be too bold. But let's put these very real issues aside for a moment and look at what Jesus actually did and asked his followers to do. Let's consider if these activities are still applicable today.

In Matthew 25:34-36, Jesus describes, in some detail what he is looking for among followers who seek to do his will:

- Feed the hungry
- Give the thirsty something to drink
- Welcome the stranger
- Clothe the needy
- Take care of the sick
- Visit the shut-in/those in prison
- Teach the Good News

In the Old Testament there is a specific call to look after the helpless—widows, orphans, handicapped, and poor.

Can we still do these today? Sure. Are there people in our community who have needs like these? Yes, there are. Can everyone contribute? Some more than others, but yes, everyone can contribute. Are there laws against doing any of these? Well, there are probably some guidelines you need to be aware of to avoid getting in trouble and we should be careful to avoid dangerous situations, but doing these things is not against the law. How do we learn more about such needs and opportunities to fulfill Jesus's expectations for us?

There are people in your community building the Kingdom by doing these things this very day. Just ask at a local church, homeless shelter, or crisis center. In a few days you will be amazed at the opportunities you can plug into. Here you can see God's will being done on earth and prayers being answered.

This is not meant to be the total story (we Christians are a contentious lot), but it can be a beginning for you. Consider it a training ground of sorts, a starting point from which God can hone your gifts and talents and more easily direct you for His good purpose.

Here is your **Reality Check: The Kingdom is being built on earth today in a big way.** I used to frequently fly around the country on business and I remember being disappointed in the church because I didn't see the Kingdom being built. I didn't see it, so I assumed it wasn't being done. As it turns out, I was just a neophyte and didn't know where to look!

> ## A Grace Moment
>
> Are you waiting to do something Big for God? Do you have a degree and an important title that tells others you are ready for big things? Maybe God is holding you in reserve for just the right time and project. Has He called you yet? Consider doing something small while you wait. Not everyone is born with a servant's heart and helping the poor and needy is not always easy. A little practice is always a good idea.

People offer financial assistance and volunteer in a big way to crisis ministries, Feed-the-Hungry programs, tutoring programs, abuse mitigation, homeless shelters, prison ministries, Meals on Wheels, clothing drives, education programs, food co-ops, food banks, etc. The list goes on and on. The Kingdom is being built in a huge way today.

People volunteer and donate, often with little recognition, to make this a better world. To eliminate all wrongs from the world? No. For money? Of course not. For recognition? Perhaps some, but for most part, no. They work humbly and quietly to make the world a better place to the glory of God. Look around. This hard to see underground economy is worth **millions** annually and provides volunteer opportunities for thousands. We can observe, verify, and establish consistency over time that God is providing opportunities (His Gift) for you to do His will on earth and to be revealed as a child of God. This is a Reality Check. There will always be opportunities for you to both give and receive for the Glory of God. Here you will consistently find God's amazing blessings and see evidence of his power on earth. This is a Reality Check you are encouraged to evaluate this week.

A word of caution. We also need to be mindful of Jesus's own humility in doing this work. After Jesus told John the Baptist's disciple all the things he had done to fulfill prophecy, Jesus added, "Blessed is he who does not fall away on my account."

This is a thought worth remembering when we have the opportunity to be the face of Jesus for others. A friend who is in Navigators told me his daily prayer was, "God, please use me as your instrument to spread the good news of Jesus Christ, and help me do it without being a jerk!" Good advice.

A Grace Moment

Am I talking "salvation through works" again? (We Christians are a contentious lot!) No! Any heathen can hand out food in a food line, and works alone will not get you into heaven. But, by the same token, if you are committed to following Christ's example, you will be about building God's Kingdom on earth.

> *So, my brothers and sisters, you also died to the law through the body of Christ, that you might belong to another, to him who was raised from the dead, in order that we might bear fruit for God.*
> —Romans 7:4

It is a matter of perspective. To see God's will being done on earth, we must look at our world from the perspective of God's Plan, having realistic expectations of what we can expect from God and what he expects from us. Then we can accept Jesus for who he is, not who we want him to be. Finally, we must work to understand ourselves and exchange our egocentric point of view to a God-centric perspective.

Let me help you make sense of how our roles work together with God and Jesus. What do we mean when we say our God is a loving God? Is His role to stand ready to save us from enemies and save those in need as the psalmist wrote? He can, but that does not seem to be what we would call His role. **He is a loving God because he is pulling for us to be revealed as children of God, worthy of an inheritance and to spend eternity with.** He does this through forgiveness and grace.

What is Jesus's role? We found that Jesus' role is to not lose any whom the father has given him and to raise them up on the last day. Likewise, our role is to help Jesus fulfill his role by helping bring people to children of God status. All three roles focus on the next life by revealing people as children of God. As we have also seen, this is not always easy. We must overcome the Human Response, the business of life, and our limited gifts and talent. Some will be more successful in their role than others, but if we all do what we can, great success is expected.

A Thoughtful Moment

Okay, I'm not too crazy about the idea of being born blind and struggling all my life only to give others the opportunity to do the right thing. It seems like a high price to pay! It is also terribly unfair!

Of course, being the instrument that helps someone into heaven is a pretty high calling. In fact, it's hard to think of a higher calling. How do you feel about being the blind person in this scenario? Have you ever been in the role of receiving before?

Also, once we accept Christ as our Lord and Savior, shouldn't God be more willing to bless us? Shouldn't life be demonstrably, consistently, and verifiably better for God's faithful followers than for non-Christians? Wouldn't prosperous, healthy Christians be a better picture of God's will being done on earth? All advances in medicine and science would come from Christians, right? Christians should be immune from persecution in the Middle East, right?

Look around at your reality. What do you think?

Several Observations on the Nature of God

Now that we have examined God's Plan, what He expects of us, what we can expect from Him and what we do as child of God, it will be helpful to take a closer look at several issues with which many of us struggle.

I once asked a wise man how can I know if the promises God made to Joshua to "never forsake Him," applied to me? He explained, "Because it is the nature of God to be consistent." God is God. He knows why He made us and what He expects from us. Further, He wants us to get to know Him. Therefore, He is consistent. So, what does God's Plan imply about His nature that we may know Him better? Let's address a couple recurring issues.

The Issue of Fairness

A problem surfaces with the issue of fairness that needs to be addressed in some depth. God has a different perspective than we have, and one difference that pops up repeatedly has to do with "fairness." Many "good" people see themselves as arbitrators between those who have and those who have not. In fact, it is difficult to argue with the benefits of those who have a lot giving to those who are in need. But let's first take a look at this desire from the perspective of God's Plan.

Here's your Reality Check: God's creation did not treat everyone fairly. Undoubtedly you have noticed that some people have it far worse than others. You may be one of them. A lot of people live in really bad circumstances. Some bring hardships upon themselves, while others are born into unfortunate situations through no fault of their own.

You may even wonder why you have it so good. Some are born prettier, wealthier, and smarter than others, and these are definite advantages in the earthly realm. Warren Buffett calls it the "Lottery of the Womb." Those lucky enough to be born to a wealthy family in the United States have a demonstrative advantage over those born to a poor family in Africa, irrespective of their innate abilities or love for God. There is no fairness here, but there is reality.

> *God's creation did not treat everyone fairly*

For those of an analytical bent, we have the Normal Distribution Curve to help explain the distribution of characteristics among populations. For example, if we group people by height, we find more people in the middle and fewer people to the taller and shorter ends of the distribution. This phenomenon is so consistent, we can make projections of height for the total population from a large enough random sample. We don't have to measure each person to make underwear. The normal distribution curve tells us how many will be size Small, Medium, Large, and X-Large. The same distribution curve can be drawn for intelligence, attractiveness, running speed, wealth, sex drive, foot size, skin color, etc. Further, it would appear that this normal distribution curve has always been so. The normal distribution curve appears to be part of God's Plan—how God created the living things on earth. When Jesus said we will always have the poor among us, he wasn't being prophetic. He was making an observation characteristic of any culture.

From the time we enter elementary school, we start assessing where we fit along many distinct normal distribution curves. We quickly have a pretty good idea of where our strengths and weaknesses fall and begin the process of reconciling our positions on a given trait versus others. If you are a slow runner, you are destined to lose a lot of foot races. So, you look for other areas in which to excel.

A Reality Check reveals that each of us knows this to be true. We are acutely aware of where we fit on normal distribution curves such as intelligence, height, looks, etc. Fair or not, we come to accept where we are and work to improve our lot by exploiting our strengths and improving upon our weaknesses. Life is not always fair, and much of this unfairness seems to be part of the design.

Shifting to the Spiritual Realm

Likewise, we may be spiritually disadvantaged from reasons of birth or from events happening to us after birth. If God is pulling for us to be revealed as children of God, why the unfair spread in blessings? On a physical plane, we accept our lot and do the best we can. On a spiritual plane, however, we are a little less sure how to interpret this reality. Is great beauty or great wealth a help or hindrance to becoming a child of God? Everyone has considered these issues, but let's get to the tougher questions. What about being born to a Hindu family in Nepal? Is the child born on the poor end of the Income Distribution Curve guilty if he steals food to eat? Is the child born to atheist parents or in a remote jungle village and never exposed to God's word, destined to hell? Is the child who has a different sexual orientation not an acceptable child to God?

These are tough questions, but you cannot get through life without dealing with at least several of them. There is a significant range of traits and abilities we judge as ranging from "God-given blessings" to "curses." However, we must deal with these when trying to understand God's Plan. Obviously, the distribution of gifts and circumstances of our birth and environment are not always "fair," but, like it or not, this is part of God's Plan. We are born where we are born and we are given the gifts we are given. We are called to deal with it and still pursue being children of God. But this only offers a partial answer to the question of fairness. Let's look deeper.

God of No Excuses

Let's examine the testimonies of two great prophets of the Old Testament on the nature of God in this regard: Jeremiah and Isaiah. Jeremiah complained to God about the difficulties of prophesying to the hardheaded Israelites of his day. The people complained about the weather (the land was parched), and things being unfair (the wicked prosper and the faithless live at ease). The hypocrites of the day praised God with their lips but kept Him far from their hearts.

Sound familiar? We can imagine Jeremiah hoping to hear God say, "What an ungrateful group! The fault lies with the people." Or, "You are doing a good job, Jeremiah. Just hang in there a little longer." Or even, "Okay, I'll send some rain."

But instead, God answered him:

> *If you have raced with men on foot and they have worn you out, how can you compete with horses? If you stumble in safe country, how will you manage in the thickets by the Jordan?*
> —Jeremiah 12:5

Not the sympathetic response Jeremiah hoped for. Is God being hard and inflexible with His servant Jeremiah? Yes, it seems He is.

Isaiah wrote:

> *Let no foreigner who has bound himself to the Lord say,*
>   *"The Lord will surely exclude me from his people."*
> *And let not any eunuch complain,*
>   *"I am only a dry tree."*
> *For this is what the Lord says:*
> *"To the eunuchs who keep my Sabbaths,*
>   *who choose what pleases me*
>   *and holds fast to my covenant—*
> *To them I will give within my temple and its walls*
>   *a memorial and a name*
>   *better than sons and daughters;*

> *I will give them an everlasting name*
> *   that will not be cut off.*
> *And foreigners who bind themselves to the Lord*
> *   to serve him,*
> *to love the name of the Lord,*
> *   and to worship him,*
> *all who keep the Sabbath without desecrating it*
> *   and who hold fast to my covenant—*
> *these I will bring to my holy mountain*
> *   and give them joy in my house of prayer.*
> —Isaiah 56:3-7

Here are two peoples with spiritual disadvantages (terribly unfair by world standards), the foreigner and the eunuch; one resulting from birth and one resulting from actions after birth. We find God's response counterintuitive but consistent throughout the Bible. God promises to treat the one born outside the family just as one born in the family. God also promises the one who is disadvantaged after birth (e.g. the eunuch) to recognize their disadvantages with a special position and recognition in heaven if they will choose what pleases God and keep his covenants. Does God condemn either group? No. But in both cases, they must do what pleases God and keep his covenants. No excuses.

Neither Jeremiah nor Isaiah give us leeway for excuses but instead focus our every effort on doing "what is pleasing to God." Jesus did not teach excuses in the name of fairness. We do not find Jesus's forgiveness where people act contrary to what is pleasing to God. Whether are born with or into disadvantages, or we have DNA with certain proclivities, we stand before God without excuse. So, the answer is this: **we must seek to do what is pleasing to God and to keep his covenants.** Despite our handicaps and unfair circumstances, we can be assured of acceptance by God, and in some cases receive special recognition for overcoming disadvantages!

We find forgiveness freely given when the repentant turn to God. We also have Jesus as a model of how to live and the Holy Spirit to intercede and guide us. But we cannot count on circumstances, clever arguments, or fairness to win Child-of-God status. Beware of those who are quick to dispense God's forgiveness in the name of fairness.

This is a hard word. We instinctively want to reject it as unfair. But where did this concept of fairness come from? Jesus lifted an obscure phrase from Leviticus (19:18), "love your neighbor as yourself," and made it our second most important commandment. This commandment places a high value on fairness as everyone wants to be treated fairly. If we love others as ourselves, we will treat them fairly. **Jesus gave us this commandment to teach us to how to live as Christians in an unfair world.**

Now that you know the answer, are you willing to accept the burdens that come with it? Knowing that God is a god of no excuses places a huge burden on Christians to reach out to, help, teach, and heal those who would use their situation as an excuse for not responding to Jesus. Are we responsible for someone else's decision to accept Jesus? No. Each person makes his own decision. But we do have an obligation (based on the Second Commandment to love/care for them) to witness by our words and actions, to help others accept Christ. If God does not accept people's excuses, even "good" excuses, for ignoring Jesus, it places a great difficulty on those who love their brothers and sisters enough to tell them about Jesus. It takes a lot of empathy to come alongside someone who is ignoring Jesus or behaving badly and convince them that God is indeed loving and caring, but will not accept their excuses for doing what is displeasing to Him.

Likewise, those in need have a huge burden to receive the word of God and respond with acceptance and love. We don't usually think of this as a burden, but of course it is. My excuses and circumstances are very real to me. My Human Response tells me so. The last thing I want to hear is that my proclivities are not significant in the bigger scheme of God's Plan.

I don't want to hear that my unfair circumstance is not a heavenly excuse. Somehow, I must be willing to change focus from excuses for rejecting God to what is pleasing to God. This is hard to do and usually requires help from those willing to be the face of Jesus for them.

A Grace Moment

One can almost hear the "extreme" arguments. But what about the autistic boy at the orphanage in Haiti? He probably does not have the mental or physical ability (severely unfair) to accept Jesus. Does God condemn him? What you call an excuse, I may call a good reason. How can you know what God will and will not accept?

"What about? What about? What about? . . ." First, who can speak for the autistic boy? Not I. Not you. When we can't articulate an answer, we now know to focus on the concept of Trust. We can trust that God, who made the heavens and the earth and who extended grace in some pretty ugly situations, undoubtedly has an answer. The key question is not about fairness. The key question is, "What about your decision?" Your decision to accept Jesus is a personal decision, not a debate.

But what of those who never heard of God or the good news of Jesus? The Apostle John included an explanation of Jesus's statement, *No one comes to the Father, except through me*, as follows:

> (Jesus speaking) *It is written in the Prophets,* (Isaiah) *"They will all be taught by God." Everyone who listens to the Father and learns from him comes to me.*
> —John 6:45

We do not know how or when this person comes to Jesus. But we trust that God does have an answer. It is comforting to know all who seek God will be taught by Him, and everyone who listens to God will have access to Jesus and Jesus will work hard not to lose any that the father sends to him. Bottom line, it is not the fine print we need to be concerned about because God's grace is sufficient whether or not we understand everything. What is important is our personal decision to accept Jesus.

A Thoughtful Moment

Take a moment to make a list describing the nature of God as you understand Him.

Now make a list for the nature of Jesus.

Finally, make a list describing your own nature.

In Praise of Hard Times

We touched on the fact that some situations can be unfair. It may be profitable to spend a little more time on the topic of Hard Times. We have genuine problems with the idea that something bad could happen for the glory of God. That is understandable. Sunday after Sunday, a loving, forgiving father figure is preached. "Come on in! It's fun and warm and you will feel better for being here! Plus, you'll meet a lot of good people." We are not taught to see our problems as opportunities for God.

The fact is, though, mankind's progress is indebted more to adversity than prosperity. Prosperity can fund the advances but filling the holes fostered by real needs, provide the muscle to propel progress. Advancements in medicine, industry, and food production are usually attributed to disease, war, and hunger. The same principle holds in the spiritual realm. We turn to God quicker in times of peril than in times of prosperity. The old saying, "There are no atheists in a foxhole," is based on this truth. Paradoxically, it's the hungry man who digs potatoes and thanks God for them while the rich man receives his potatoes without appreciation. It's during the hard times we look for the face of Jesus. We can call this human response a spiritual gift.

Reality Check: We grow more in tough times, so let's learn to embrace them. I came to Christ kicking and screaming at the age of thirty-two. Raised in a Christian home, I attended church but never knew the reality of God until I came face-to-face with the overwhelming problem of being laid off with a new family and numerous monthly bills. Out of desperation and on my knees, I finally turned to God. It was only when I realized I could not make it on my own that I came to trust Jesus. I did not have anything against Jesus or the church, I just did not have time to focus on either. Today I am thankful for being laid off, and even the incredible stress it wrought. Otherwise, I am convinced I would have never known the Reality of God. Worry about this life and the pursuit of wealth competes with Jesus for our time and makes us unfruitful. In Matthew 13:22, Jesus called this the "deceit of wealth."

During the good times, there is the natural tendency to say, "I did well," or, "Look what I accomplished," as

> *We grow more in tough times*

opposed to praising God. It is only after we hit bottom and recover that we become boldly generous and think, "How will this problem be used to glorify God?"

It has always been so. The earth is designed to give us opportunities to learn to trust God. As a result, mankind has the choice to claim credit for successes and curse God for his failures, or trust God and praise Him for all.

Why would God's plan call for us to go through hardship and disappointment? This is a hard question. When I get to heaven, I'll ask Him. Perhaps it is our stubborn self-focus and pleasure-seeking ways. Perhaps it is our argumentative and contentious nature. Knowing our Human Response, could we really trust a faith that was not tested? Probably not.

A Grace Moment

Consider for a moment having the option to change God's Plan so that you have more control over your circumstances versus relying on His grace and mercy to help you achieve Child-of-God status. Would you make the change?

A Word of Encouragement

It is impossible to understand Jesus's work in our lives if we do not understand what he is after. We think Jesus is here to guide us and then find ourselves hopelessly lost in processes like divorce or unemployment.

We think Jesus is here to bless us and then we wake up to learn our investments have disappeared and our life is in turmoil. When we are dying, we pray to Jesus to heal us only to recall his moment in Gethsemane just before he went to the cross.

Tough times have purpose in our lives as we develop the faith and trust of children. But God is pulling for us. He hopes, expects, and anticipates that we will be revealed as children of God. Therefore, it is more accurate and rewarding to see the struggles as an opportunity to prepare for our role.

Patience is required

Reality Check: We can't know who or when God chooses someone to be His child until their life has ended. Our role as children of God therefore requires great patience.

Outsiders can look at Christians and think, "Steer clear of these conflicted people!"

Christians can look strange when they weave back and forth in prayer and song. Christians struggle mightily to describe their faith, often using strange phrases. They can even sound like hypocrites when trying to use examples. We suspect this has always been so.

Is this faith all foolishness, mass hypnosis, hysteria, or a hollow hope? Of course not. Waste not a minute on such questions! When literally billions of people confess to the same truth over the centuries, when someone you know who would not lie to you tells you about the Reality of Jesus, stop asking foolish questions and start asking God to come into your life. Do not get sidetracked by differences in people's experience and backgrounds. Who can fully know God?

People are different and we see those differences reflected in the many denominations, service formats, and rituals. This is okay. It is wonderful we have the freedom to express our faith in ways that are most meaningful to us. Let us learn to praise God for the faith people **do** have. This praise is a good start.

Remember, most believers were non-believers first. Further, it may well take Jesus our entire life to correct misconceptions and erroneous teaching, and that's okay too.

Indeed, why would we expect everyone to like the same hymn or find the same significance in worship experiences? Would you expect to hear the same report from four hundred tourists who went to Spain? Of course not! We would hear of the olive groves from the farmers, the appeal of quaint roads disappearing over the gentle rise of the countryside from the romantic, and the ancient walls that capture the imagination of the historian. People are different. We have different backgrounds, experiences, and interests, and our story is shaped by these differences. A vacationer may decide to visit Spain after hearing about one event and another decides to go after a lifetime of study. People are different and that is okay.

A Grace Moment

Do you ever find yourself growing contentious over the errors other people make in worshipping God? Most people do. Instead, try praising God for the unmerited grace required for each of us. And praise Him for the faith we do have. At least it's a beginning.

Be humbled at the very idea of man's struggles to know the mind of God. You can even delight in the inconsistencies and fervor of those struggling to know God better just as you would show patience with the young. A toddler struggling to master the course from the crib to the dressing table can look pretty funny. But it is through these very struggles we learn to walk, run, dance, and leap for joy.

Likewise, a wise person may seek to know God for a number of reasons. When you see someone making fun of Christians, think back to Paul's Damascus Road experience in Acts. Better still, remember your attitude before you came to know Jesus and be patient with the scoffer! Remember most people were non-believers before they became Christians and there are billions of Christians today.

Patience is Also Required for Church Leaders

Christianity is flourishing in many parts of the world but it is declining in the United States. The secularization of our institutions and a hostile media have taken a toll, particularly on the young. Church leaders are often poorly trained to confront secular teaching in public schools or address conflicting social trends. Further, church members are increasingly hostile to church leadership for not teaching them how to respond to their children's questions or to public questioning of their faith. It is frustrating and embarrassing, and church leaders often get the blame. Church leaders can also catch flak for taking a stand. Church members, seeking to feel progressive and avoid embarrassment, may buy into secular arguments of fairness, thereby pulling the rug out from under their leaders who try to articulate Christian principles. It's a tough job. Church leaders need our prayers, support, and encouragement more than ever. They also need for us to maintain Christian standards and values.

A Thoughtful Moment

One of the most frustrating passages in the Bible is found in Job. Job poses the rhetorical question to his friends:

> *Who is the Almighty that we should serve him? What would we gain by praying to him?*
> —Job 21:15

I really wanted God to answer that question. Instead God ended the book with His, "I am that I am," speech. Did God miss a great opportunity to tell Job and us why we should follow Him? Do you think God should have explained Himself a little better? How does this passage relate to the idea of Great Patience?

Concluding Remarks

After first being exposed to God's Plan, a disconnect emerges between what we were taught as children and what we observe and read in the Bible. By focusing on what we can observe and by studying the Bible, a plan, a relationship, and a purpose emerges that makes more sense. It's not the plan most of us would have written or chosen, but as we can see, God's plan does appear to be both good and clever. Because it focuses on God's Plan instead of our plan, it is easier to understand how our faith has resisted extinction and even prospered for thousands of years.

God's Plan is for us to be revealed as His children, worthy of an inheritance and desirable to spend eternity with. While we want everything to be about our plans, it's not. God's creation and our temporal bodies are part of His plan. He is pulling for us and giving us every opportunity to choose Him. God stacks the deck in our favor but that doesn't mean our fate is a foregone conclusion. We have to deal with the "gifts" God gave us.

God sent Jesus with a specific mission to save everyone God gave him and to raise them up on the last day. We can help Jesus fulfill his mission by accepting our role to do God's will on earth. Jesus is active today. We just have to know where to look! We can see God's will being done on earth if we just look. We can witness prayers being answered when we pray in Jesus's name, for His will to be done to the Glory of God. We can see amazing things accomplished and lives changed when we accept our role and work toward God's will.

Jesus is active today

Godly leaders in the Bible seemed to understand their role and this relationship to God. They built their lives around doing God's will, fulfilling their mission, in order to please God. They sometimes stumbled, backtracked, complained and grumbled, but they knew what God expected of them. Today, many seem to have lost this fundamental understanding, somehow thinking it's about us.

We have to know where to look!

God is God and it is up to us to be revealed as His children, worthy of an inheritance and desirable to spend eternity with. We can't buy salvation, we can't gain it by prayer alone, we can't gain it by works alone, and we can't gain it by just being good. We can't even wait till the last minute to turn to Jesus because we don't know when the last minute might be. We can't blame God. We can't blame our parents or guardians or teachers or preachers or bosses. We can't cry unfair. We can't even blame our genes. **God is a god of no excuses.**

We have to put aside what we learned as children and accept responsibility for our time on earth. We must see God's gifts, both physical and spiritual, as opportunities to glimpse God's will for us and to use them for His glory. We can know He will bless our efforts to use His gifts for His glory because that is the nature of God. Further, His gifts are not playthings to be toyed with and discarded or used inappropriately. God's gifts are to be claimed and used to His glory!

When we pray in His name, we pray for strength and perseverance to do His will and for protection from the evil one. While we work in response to this prayer, we can expect God's blessings to get the task accomplished. There are many examples of God's amazing plans in the bible and we hear of examples even today.

It is okay to pray in your name for God's blessings. It is natural and in the spirit of a child to do so. But we must not be disappointed or disillusioned when this prayer is not answered because this prayer may be contrary to God's will for us.

Gird Yourself for Faith

We have Jesus. We have the Holy Spirit. We have the Bible. We have little need for contentious debate among Christians. We can learn to praise God for the faith our brothers and sisters do have and try to contribute to their maturation. This bears repeating: **most people were non-believers before they became believers.** God has given us an entire lifetime to freely turn to him. Contentious debate therefore makes little sense. Encouragement does.

God delights in our freely turning to Him. Jesus and the Holy Spirit can direct your paths if you are willing. Jesus said:

> *Because I live, you may live also.*
> —John 14:19

Let our faith in a living Jesus be sufficient to love and be patient with one another even to the fullness of their life. God will accept their turning to Him even at the end of life, so don't be discouraged if someone you care about has not accepted Jesus yet. As long as there is life, there is hope.

Because we are an argumentative lot and subject to public pressure, let me suggest three things to focus on. Educate ourselves well enough to be able to reject false teaching and bad leadership. We know that even the Devil can quote scripture and pervert its meaning. We are used to people misrepresenting the Bible to support their arguments. It takes time to study the Bible and pray for discernment, but this is not a hard thing to do. Start today.

Second, protect your children and teach them the fundamentals of your faith. If you leave it up to others, it will not get done. We learn a sad lesson from the Old Testament:

> *Within one generation after Joshua's generation died, another generation grew up who knew neither the Lord nor what he had done for Israel.*
> —Judges 2:10

Key values of faith, work, perseverance, family, honesty, integrity, respect, trust, heritage, value, delayed gratification, and stewardship make our life better and are worthy of both protection and teaching to our children.

Further, parents must protect their children both physically and spiritually from those vested in teaching them about tolerance against God's teachings and values. You would not let your fourteen-year-old daughter go out with a twenty-one-year-old man, and you must not turn your young children over to those who would take advantage of their youth. This sounds hard because you may have to verbally reject someone else's teaching to protect your child. Some hesitate to do this because it is confrontational. But your child is worth it. (Remember the warning not to be a jerk.) Teach your child that if you really love your neighbor as yourself, then you will care about their soul more than temporarily hurting their feelings. If you do not reject their erroneous teaching, you put a stumbling block in their path to repenting, and without repentance, there is no salvation. Teach your child to truly care about another's soul and not be responsible for putting stumbling blocks in their path to salvation. You do not have to be a jerk to teach what you believe.

Then we stand ready to protect our family. Cowering to agnostic civil leaders and liberal minorities as our country slid into a Post-Christian era was a poor witness and unattractive to potential believers. **You will be damaged by insidious cynicism if you are passive.** When called hate-mongers, Christians must respond, "No, Christianity is about love, not hate." Our second greatest commandment is, *Thou shall love your neighbor as yourself.* You must be willing and able to defend what you believe. Jesus's great defense-of-marriage speech in the Gospel of Mark was, to my knowledge, never brought up during the recent debates on marriage. Studying the bible does not appear to be a priority these days.

Third, take stock of the fruit you are producing. Talk to your spouse or close friend. Have a private conversation with Jesus. Take a hard look at your prayer life. Are your prayers in your name or Jesus's name?

Don't Reject Faith

We live in unreasonable times. People don't like restrictions of any kind and tend to reject those they can unless there is a clear personal benefit. It is our Human Response. We don't like someone telling us what to do. But we do understand cooperation. When the garbage piles up on the lot next door; everyone agrees neighbors should put their garbage away. Similarly, many are afraid following God will result in unwanted restrictions on their freedom, but they do want to live in a better world. Let us cooperate for a good purpose.

But do cooperate wisely. We want to feel good about ourselves and avoid criticism. Many prefer high-minded theories to experience even though we know—as Aristotle pointed out long ago—that in the competition for success, experience wins out over theory due to the critical nature of execution. We are dismayed when rhetoric triumphs over logic to everyone's detriment. Despite millions of testimonies from serious and competent people, study of our faith is rejected by many in favor of weak theories lacking in experience.

This reluctance to learn about Jesus due to bad theory is bolstered by our Human Response, and as a result, we live in a cynical world. It's important to recognize that cynicism has a purpose: to undermine progress and foster hopelessness.

Cynicism is like a sore, making it uncomfortable to move forward. Letting an opponent give you a sore to slow or stop you can be very effective. Consider the college professor who taught his students that God did not exist, and that every culture created a god to explain things they could not otherwise explain. This cynical sore slows the student's progress and potentially influences their beliefs to be compatible with the cynic's own. The wise person seeks out experience.

In 1985, I stood on a street corner with a businessman in Guatemala and we examined a machine gun nest on the other side of the street. Fighter jets flew overhead to attack guerillas up north near the Mexican border. He explained that a man of the people would arise and take control in Guatemala and everyone would have great hope for things to get better. Each time that man became as corrupt as the one before, and the process would begin anew. It was so disappointing for the people of Guatemala. Many felt hopeless. Fortunately, with practice, the Human Response, as well as cynicism, can be recognized and rejected for what they are.

Focus on the Question

If we ask or respond to the wrong question, we are apt to reach the wrong conclusion. We often lose an argument before we get started by responding to the wrong question. Questions of fairness and propriety seem to be particularly confusing these days. You will do well to address the topic by asking yourself, "What is pleasing to God?" You will often be surprised by the answer, but work to accept the answer the Holy Spirit gives you.

We've explored one simple question in this book: "Is the Lord's Prayer being answered?" I pray that this journey has been fruitful for you. I encourage you to ask the tough questions about your faith and go to the Bible in prayer for answers. Millions of testimonies over thousands of years obviate any doubts about there being answers. Indeed, you can be assured there are answers. Be also assured by the heritage and testimony of your faith that they will be good answers, but be open to the idea that the answers may surprise you. Most of all: **Be careful how you listen!**

Epilogue

This book is short for a reason. I referenced as few Biblical characters and used as few examples and testimonies as possible to illustrate a few key points. I even tried to avoid jargon and the space required to define it so you could get through the book quickly and start or renew your journey in the Bible. The Bible provides a language and references that allow God to speak directly to you and to answer the questions you need answered. This is an incredibly rewarding adventure.

But it is not easy. I recommend a bible with great indexes, references, and explanations, like the *Life Application Bible, New International Version.* Take your time. Read your Bible through, join a bible study group. Become familiar with the stories and characters. Most importantly, explore the references and take time to read the notes. You will be well rewarded for the extra effort.

Afterwards, when you have questions, you are better able to hear God when he gives you instructions on where to look. Indexes and references will allow you to quickly research several passages for the answer you seek. BibleGateway.com is an excellent online resource. When you come to the answer God is leading you to, you will know it in your heart. You will know the answer is one you can count on. It is an incredibly exciting process and I wish you much success.

By way of example, I was struggling with the Trilemma—how can an all-knowing, all-powerful, and loving God allow terrible things to happen?—when I was led to Paul's explanation in Romans 8:19-24. I had researched a number of passages, but knew instantly Romans 8 was where God was leading me. Still, the passage did not yield a clear answer. It took rearranging sentences; Paul's scholarly logic flows differently than our contemporary language, plus studying several translations before arriving at a full understanding of what God wanted me to see. Even when I had the answer I sought, I was challenged by other people's experience with the same passage, which, remember, is okay.

My minister at the time, a respected scholar, said, "No. This passage is about hope." Which of course it is, but stopping there missed the foundational truth the Apostle Paul used in making his point on hope: *As surely as God has a plan for us, we have hope.* The answer I was seeking was in the truism Paul used to make his point about hope: **God has a plan for us.**

Rejoice in the freedom and incredible opportunity you have to ask questions, get answers and to learn what God wants to teach you. Be bold and do not become discouraged. And always be careful how you listen.

Notes

Unless otherwise noted, bible verses are taken from the *Life Application Bible: New International Version.*

Page 10: Read more about Reflex Sympathetic Dystrophy Syndrome: https://rsdfoundation.org/crps.html.

Page 14: Refresh your memory of Jesus's struggle with the cup of the crucifixion at Matthew 26:39, "My Father, if it is possible, may this cup be taken from me. Yet not as I will, but as you will."

Page 16: Different translations add to our understanding of God's Plan. In verse 20, Creation is subjected to "frustration" (NIV), "futility" (New King James). In verse 19, the creation "eagerly awaits" (New King James), "breathless anticipation" (Common English), "in hopes" (NIV) for the children of God to be revealed.

Page 42-43: Human Response. Read about followers looking to Jesus for free food in John 6:22-27.

Page 45: Refresh your memory of the exciting story of Jesus raising Lazarus from the dead in John 11, 12:12-27.

Page 60: "A wise business man." John Holland was CEO of Fruit of the Loom, and a highly respected business leader when I met him in the early 1980s. I never met with Mr. Holland without learning something valuable about management and life.

Page 65: ". . . without being a jerk!" Tom Perkins was last person college classmates would have guessed would dedicate his life to serving Jesus. Amazing story.

Page 69: "I asked a wise man . . ." I heard Bob Pettus speak at a New Canaan Meeting one morning and was so impressed, I called to ask his advice on a couple issues I was struggling with. He was a generous and genuinely caring person. Bob died in 2004.

You can learn more about New Canaan Society at http://www.newcanaansociety.org/

Page 95: We've had a tendency to place hope in exciting new theories, but Aristotle pointed out a long time ago, "We see those of experience succeeding more than those who have theory without experience. The reason for this is that experience is knowledge of particulars and actions, and the effects produced, are all concerned with the particular."

A Word from the Author

I came to Christ kicking and screaming at the age of thirty-two. In my younger life, I was committed to pursuing the New, the Exciting, and the Challenging. Finally, I found all these in Jesus.

Prayer, Bible study, and a quest for understanding led me on a forty-year journey to understand how my faith works. In 2002, I came to the decision to submit to writing what I had learned. After another twenty years of editing, expanding and purging, I found others had many of the same questions, and committed to publishing a small book in hopes of helping new Christians on their walk.

I'd love to hear from you. Please send your comments to cbforrest129@gmail.com, or visit www.realitycheckforrest.com for the latest news. Unless specified otherwise, your feedback may be shared with potential readers.

Some names in this text have been changed out of considerations for privacy.

Charles Forrest lives with his wonderful wife of forty years in Winston-Salem, North Carolina. He has an adventurous daughter who is making the world a better place, and a talented son. Charles enjoys reading, teaching, fishing and skiing.

www.ingramcontent.com/pod-product-compliance
Lightning Source LLC
Chambersburg PA
CBHW020301010526
44108CB00037B/481